Uprooting Every Demonic Prophecy

DELIVERANCE SERIES VOLUME 12

Bishop Climate Irungu

Contents

False Prophets

I will raise them up a Prophet from among their brethren, like unto thee, and will put my words in his mouth, and he shall speak unto them all that I shall command him. And it shall come to pass, that whosoever will not hearken unto my words which he shall speak in my name, I will require it of him. But the prophet, which shall presume to speak a word in my name, which I have not commanded him to speak, or that shall speak in the name of other gods, even that prophet shall die. And if thou say in thine heart, How shall we know the word which the LORD hath not spoken? When a prophet speaketh in the name of the LORD, if the thing follow not, nor come to pass, that is the thing which the LORD hath not spoken, but the prophet hath spoken it presumptuously: thou shalt not be afraid of him.

(Deuteronomy 18:18-22)

Therefore hearken not ye to your prophets, nor to your diviners, nor to your dreamers, nor to your enchanters, nor to your sorcerers, which speak unto you, saying, Ye shall not serve the king of Babylon: For they prophesy a lie unto you, to remove you far from your land, and that I should drive you out, and ye should perish.

(Jeremiah 27:9-10)

PART ONE

What is a Demonic Prophecy?

Today, many people underestimate the power of words. Just take a walk on the street and you'll see how carelessly words are tossed around. Curses are being released every day and we render it to mere statements; not knowing it has the power to change our lives. But if we're going to have victory in this life then we must understand what words are.

Words are spirit; they are not physical. They are vehicles – used to deliver a message. They carry authority, weight and power. And words are seeds.

The Bible says in Proverbs 18:22,

"The power of life and death is in the tongue".

When someone speaks over your life those words are planted as a seed; whether good or bad. But many of us allow people to speak into our lives, even cursing us, and we just laugh it off. Not realizing that a seed has already been sown. Not realizing that a demonic prophecy has been released over our lives.

What is a demonic prophecy? Simply put, a demonic prophecy is a declaration made over one's life that is intended for evil.

There are many prophets in the world but how can we know if they are from God? The Bible says,

"I will raise them up a Prophet from among their brethren, like unto thee, and will put my words in his mouth; and he shall speak unto them all that I shall command him. And it shall come to pass, that whosoever will not hearken unto my words which he shall speak in my name, I will require it of him. But the prophet, which shall presume to speak a word in my name, which I have not commanded him to speak, or that shall speak in the name of other gods, even that prophet shall die. And if thou say in thine heart, How shall we know the word which the LORD hath not spoken? When a prophet speaketh in the name of the LORD, if the thing follow not, nor come to pass, that *is* the thing which the LORD hath not spoken, *but* the prophet hath spoken it presumptuously: thou shalt not be afraid of him".

(Deuteronomy 18:18-22)

The Bible says that any prophet who speaks a word in God's name which he has not been commanded to speak shall die. The word for 'die' here is the same word used in Genesis 2:17 when God told Adam that if he ate of the tree of knowledge of good and evil he would surely die. We all know that Adam didn't die physically after eating from the tree but he did die spiritually. There was a separation from God. His life became a life of struggle; there was no more divine favour; there was no more divine protection but he had to work for everything on his own.

There are many prophets today that are already

dead; spiritually dead. They are separated and disconnected from God. Which means whatever they speak into your life, because they are already dead, it will bring death. It may even sound like a positive prophecy but when they speak, they are speak death. No life can come from them because they are already separated from God. And any prophecy that you receive from them into your life is not going to bring you closer to your miracle but it will take you farther away.

Jeremiah spoke about it.

Therefore hearken not ye to your prophets, nor to your diviners, nor to your dreamers, nor to your enchanters, nor to your sorcerers, which speak unto you, saying, Ye shall not serve the king of Babylon: For they prophesy a lie unto you, to remove you far from your land; and that I should drive you out, and ye should perish.

(Jeremiah 27:9-10)

There are people with a private agenda. Prophets that stand in the name of the Lord but when they open up their mouth all they do is prophesy lies.

They are full of ego, acting as prophets or prophetesses, causing chaos in people's lives. Others are devils agents working undercover to release spells over your life through their prophecies; before you find out your life is ruined. Others are full of jealousy and envy so they use that opportunity to curse you. And for what purpose? To remove you from your land and to drive you out so that you perish.

There are so many people today that have been removed from their blessing and removed from their land because of demonic prophecy. Demonic prophecy only serves one purpose, to uproot you from your blessing; to uproot you from your destiny; to put you in a demonic circle, chasing after something that never leads to anything. Demonic prophecies even turn you against God because anyone not fulfilling the plans of God for their lives are actually fighting against God.

You need to be careful about who you allow to speak into your life. We all love prophecy. Who doesn't want a word from God? But many of us, whenever we hear a prophecy, we just pick it up and receive it into our lives without even confirming where it is really coming from. Because there are people who have been assigned by the enemy to destroy your life. Their job is only one, to uproot you from your land.

In the days of Jeremiah, there were people under demonic assignment. Their job was to make sure that Israel would be dismantled. To make sure that the nation of Israel would never rise up again. They prophesied to the children of Israel but they were working for the enemy to try and make them miss their blessing. And it is the same thing that is happening today. Demonic prophecies are designed to take away your blessing. They have been assigned by the enemy to make sure you leave what God has for you. But every demonic prophecy over your life I command it to be exposed right now in the name of Jesus.

You see, if you want to destroy somebody's vision, you don't take their vision away. Human beings have been designed in such a way to work by replacement. When you want to get rid of a habit you have to replace it with something else. Otherwise it won't be too long before you are naturally forced back into that habit. So what you do is create a division; another vision. The enemy knows that if he takes away your vision, you will go back to it. So when he wants to mess you up, what he does is introduce another vision into your life. Similar to the original but different enough to throw you off track. And then you end up following a vision that is not from God.

There are people with the gift to see into your life. And some saw that you were the star in the family, so instead of blessing you they cursed you by releasing a demonic prophesy over your life. Because of jealousy, they sentenced you to the wilderness for the rest of your life. That's why you begin to see people getting involved in businesses that God hasn't called them to or going after things they haven't been appointed to. I'm talking about people quitting their jobs to come and serve in full-time ministry when that is not what God has called them to do. There are people whom God has anointed as business men to be able to support the work of God but you find them striving to preach because someone prophesied over their lives and that prophecy wasn't even from God. Child of God, you will only find success in the place of your anointing.

Demonic prophesies are meant to uproot you from the plans that God has for your life. To put you in a wilderness far, far away from where you're supposed to be. The Bible says 'they prophesy lies unto you in order to remove you far from your land'. Their job is to detour you; to send you away from God's blessing in your life. Demonic prophesies make you feel good, thinking you are being sent in the right direction, but you end up in the wilderness. And the problem with demonic prophecy is that it makes you cocky. It makes you proud. You think that no one can tell you otherwise because you have 'heard from God'. Meanwhile it was the devil. And in reality, you have been sentenced to the wilderness; financial wilderness, marital wilderness, etc. But that is not your portion in the name of Jesus.

The spirit of the prophet is subject to the prophet.

For ye may all prophesy one by one, which all may learn, and all may be comforted. And the spirits of the prophets are subject to the prophets. For God is not the author of confusion, but of peace, as in all churches of the saints.

(1 Coronthians 14:31-33)

The problem here is that you have attached yourself to different prophets and you hold onto them for guidance and direction thinking that they are the mouth of God over your life. But when they prophesy, instead of being moved by the Holy Spirit, they are moved by evil spirits. That is why nothing is working in your life anymore. Because that prophesy, instead of planting you it uproots you. It uproots you from your land; it uproots you from your job; it uproots you from your marriage. And you end up going in another direction in which you perish. You could have been very successful, you could have chosen the right career but you allowed someone to speak into your life and it messed up everything.

Understand that when God wants to bless you He will bring people into your life. And when the devil wants to destroy you he will also bring people into your life.

One day I met a man from Nigeria, a prominent businessman; a highly educated man who worked for Central Bank. But one day, desperate for a word from God, he began to visit some prophets. And he would listen and receive their prophecies into his life. Suddenly, the man began having nightmares. And everything in his life started going downhill. His job, his finances, everything became stagnant. He went from one problem to another, all because of demonic prophecy. And don't get me wrong; these prophets were born-again Christians. But they were already dead; moved by the devil instead of the Spirit of God. When I spoke to that man and told him to cut himself off from those prophets. Instantly, once he stopped receiving their prophecy, everything began to stabilize. There was no more harassment in his working place; he was even promoted to assistant director.

Child of God, people can speak into your lives but you need to bind every idle tongue that lifts itself against you. When you accept and receive a prophecy, you give it the power to come to pass in your life; whether it is from God or not.

I met a young girl from Vienna who came to me for prayer regarding a constant pain she had in her lower back. And she began to tell me how one day a certain man of God spoke to her and prophesied that there was an evil mark on her back that had been put there by the devil. She received what he said, thinking it was just a revelation from God. But soon after, she began experiencing a sharp pain in the same spot the prophet had spoken of. There had been nothing wrong with her before but once that man spoke over her life, he released a demonic prophecy and because she received it it came to pass. But I prayed and rebuked that pain and it left in the name of Jesus.

PART TWO

Four Signs That You Are Under Demonic Prophecy

1. Confusion

When you find yourself ready to make a huge decision in life, confusion will come in order to cause you to miss your opportunity. Every time a blessing is coming your way, the enemy will blow a wind of confusion so that you never receive it. You end up starting something but never finishing it. You get so close to your breakthrough but then confusion comes and you have to start all over again.

2. Night Attacks

The Bible says in Matthew 13:25 that 'while men slept the enemy came and sowed tares'. For some of us the enemy has been sowing fear at night. You wake up sweating; your heart beating so fast; but yet you can't even remember what you were dreaming about. You have terrifying visions, dreams of seeing strange things, snakes, people chasing you, etc.

3. Surprise

Things that you never expected begin to show up. You begin hearing things that make your jaw drop. Sometimes you apply for something and you get something else. You always find that what you get is not what you wanted. It seems as though there is someone behind the scenes making all the decisions for you and the decisions are opposite to what you want. But it is an evil hand stealing your blessing. Just like Jacob worked seven years for Rachel and Laban tricked him by giving him Leah in the night. There are hands working in the night, causing confusion, so that you always end up with the wrong thing. There is an evil hand that is always exchanging your blessing.

4. Reduced Results

When a demonic prophecy is released into your life you begin to detour from the road God has mapped for you. That is when you experience reduced results. You never achieve what you really desire. When a weed grows with a plant it will choke the real seed; sucking up all the nutrients so the plant never fully develops. That is what demonic prophecies do. They suck your destiny. They reduce you from what you are supposed to be. You begin experiencing a choke in other areas of your life as well; finances, career, marriage, etc. You work so hard but nothing seems to manifest because something is choking it. Sometimes you can even feel as though you are being physically choked.

Child of God, I know that you have been in a situation where you were so desperate for a word from God; so desperate for a sense of direction; so desperate for something to be confident in. But let me tell you, the enemy used that desperation to destroy you. That is why nothing in your life is working. Nothing is progressing. Struggle is all you know. You have been sentenced to wilderness by demonic prophecy. But right now I declare that every demonic prophecy that has ever been spoken over your life is broken in the name of Jesus. Some of you have been sent so far away; you are already in the desert. You don't even know what to do anymore; you are just wandering. But I declare over your life that God is about to guide you back to your rightful place. God is about to guide you back to your favour; to guide you back to your blessing.

Some of you received demonic prophecies while you were still in your mother's womb, others when you were young. Someone full of demonic venom spoke over your life and set you on a lifetime of failure. But I hear the Lord saying that according to Joel 2:25 "He is going to restore all the years that the locust has eaten". I command you to stop wandering and to get back to your promised land in the name of Jesus. A season is coming where you are going to enjoy prosperity again. You will enjoy favour again; you will enjoy success again.

Some of you went and visited some evil prophets. They took your name, put it in a bottle, and threw it into the water. Ever since then, as long as it is afloat, your life has no direction. But I send angels right now to go pick up that bottle in the name of Jesus.

Your enemies have been waiting. Harvest time has come, and they are expecting you to harvest tares but I declare you will take those tares and burn them so that you experience the true harvest God prepared for you before the foundations of the world. Your enemies will be waiting but they are going to be surprised when they look at your field and see what God has for you. Their plan has failed. The days of suffering are over. I know that people have been laughing at you; nothing you try has been working. But it's not over yet. Now it is harvest time. We are going to uproot every demonic prophecy over your life. We are going to bind it and set it on fire in the name of Jesus!

There is someone reading this book and the Spirit of God is revealing to me that someone full of jealousy has released a demonic prophecy over your life; that is why things are failing everywhere. You need to be delivered; you need to be set free. Someone else I can see that a demonic prophecy has been released over your life through witchcraft to hinder you and your family. But today in the name of Jesus you are going to be free! There is someone else reading this book; I hear in my spirit that you have tried so much to be free, but until all the demonic prophecies are uprooted and destroyed out of your life, nothing is going to change. Today I want you to make a point to contact me. Today you can begin your deliverance by using the special Prayer Points I have prepared for you and follow the instructions that I have given in the next few pages. It is very important that you follow them because every demonic prophecy over your life must be destroyed now. I see you victorious. I see you as a winner in the name of Jesus Christ!

Uproot Every Demonic Prophecy

Before you pray, remember to put on the full armor of God according to Ephesians 6:10-18, touching each part of your body as you say it.

Repeat with me: "I put on the full armor of God. The helmet of salvation upon my head, the breastplate of righteousness in its place, the belt of truth around my waist, my feet shod with the readiness of the gospel of peace, taking the shield of faith in my left hand and the sword of the spirit in my right".

In the Name of Jesus:

1. I take authority over all the powers, all the principalities, every ruler, and every evil spirit in high places. Satan the blood of Jesus is against you

2. Every demonic prophecy that has been released over my life, I command it to die by fire!

3. Every demonic prophecy that has sentenced me to the wilderness, I break its powers in the name of Jesus!

4. Every demonic prophecy that has sentenced me to sickness, confusion, poverty, and singleness, I break its powers in the name of Jesus!

5. Whatsoever has been sucking my destiny, draining my finances, draining my emotions, draining my profit, I command it to die by fire in the name of Jesus!

6. Every tare that has been sown into my life that is choking my destiny, choking my finances, choking my marriage, choking my peace, I command it do die by fire!

7. Every demonic prophecy that is causing delay and failure in my life, I command it to die by fire!

8. Anything that is not of God in my life, financially, physically, spiritually, or socially, I uproot it in the name of Jesus! I command it to die by fire!

9. Every demonic prophecy that has released death in my life, my finances, my children, my marriage, my career, my business, I command it to die by fire!

10. I take authority over every demonic decree that has been released over my life; I render it helpless and powerless over every area of my life in the name of Jesus!

11. Every demonic prophecy that has been released against my life through witchcraft I command it to die by fire!

12. Every demonic prophecy that has been activated to hinder my progress, I command it to die by fire in the name of Jesus Christ!

13. Every demonic prophecy that was spoken over me as result of jealousy, I uproot it right now out of my life and family in the name of Jesus!

14. Every demonic prophecy over my marriage, I command it to die by fire!

15. Every demonic prophecy over my children, I command it to die by fire!

16. Every demonic prophecy over my body that has been causing abnormalities, I command it to die by fire!

17. Every demonic prophecy over the works of my hands that has resulted in bad luck and failure, I command it to die by fire!

18. Every demonic prophecy that has been spoken against our church, I command it to die by fire in the name of Jesus!

19. Every demonic prophecy that has been released against me to terminate my destiny, to terminate my career, I command it to die by fire in the name of Jesus!

20. Every demonic prophecy that has been ruling my life, causing confusion and frustration, I command it to die by fire in the name of Jesus!

CONCLUSION

What Can I Expect?

So now that you have your prayer points you need to understand that deliverance is not a onetime event but a process and you need to be consistent if you are going to destroy the enemies in your life. Let's look at a few things you can expect while going through your deliverance.

Firstly, expect to be set free and for peace to return back into your life. The Bible says that those who wait for the Lord shall not be ashamed. Also, start expecting God to give you a testimony, just like everyone else who has gone through our deliverance program.

There are some key steps you can follow to ensure you are doing everything properly in order to obtain your desired goals. (These are in addition to your daily prayer points listed in this book)

1. Locate the area of your need

According to what your situation may be, you need to identify the particular area, or areas, which are most dire.

2. Find out what the Word of God says regarding that area

Select the appropriate scriptures promising you what you desire and meditate upon them. Write them on your walls where you can see them. Even if it means writing it on yourself so you won't forget to recite them during the day. Do whatever it takes but make sure you are replaying them in your mind daily.

3. Exercise one of the following prayers while expecting your deliverance

· 3 day Night Vigil at the Sanctuary (i.e. praying and confessing the Word from 10 pm to 5 am for 3 nights in a row)

· 3 Day Fast (i.e. praying, fasting, and confessing the Word daily from 6 am to 6 pm for 3 days. Alternatively you can fast straight through the 3 days only breaking for communion)

· 3-Day Fasting & Prayer Vigil at the Sanctuary (i.e. praying, fasting, and confessing the Word daily from 10 am to 6 pm for 3 days. Again you can fast continually for 3 days apart from communion)

· 3+ Days Dry Fast (i.e. praying, fasting, and confessing the Word for 3 or more days without taking food or drink). Please note: This should only be done under pastoral recommendation.

4. Pray aggressively while believing that you receive your deliverance

Hebrews 11:6 says, *"We must believe that He is and that He is a rewarder of them that diligently seek Him"*.

5. Make any adjustments in your life and repent as the Holy Spirit leads

You have to make sure that you are not leaving any open doors for the enemy to regain access in your life.

6. This is the most crucial step. You must sow your seed to seal your deliverance

Most people sow consecutive seeds, giving it the same name according to their expectation from God regarding their deliverance. To truly succeed in spiritual warfare you have to be a sower. The Bible says in Deuteronomy 16:16 to "never appear before God empty handed". So as you are expecting to receive something from God you need to be giving back something to Him as well.

7. Lastly, prepare yourself for your miracle physically and spiritually

Be vigorous in attending service as much as possible in order to receive the ministration of the Word and the laying on of the hands by the man of God. Also, attend your deliverance sessions regularly if you have been assigned to a mentor.

Bishop Climate Ministries
P.O. Box 67884, London, SE5 9JJ
England, United Kingdom
Tel: +44 7984 115900
Email: partners@bishopclimate.org

Yes Bishop! I want to come into agreement with you that as I sow my seed of Deliverance according to THE NUMBER OF MY AGE, I believe every demonic prophecy over my life is uprooted and destroyed in the name of Jesus!

£ _____

Please also send me: Anointed Oil for Total Victory

Here is my Prayer request covering the 7 areas I desire the Lord to manifest His Miracles in my life:

_____
_____
_____
_____
_____
_____
_____

(Continued on Back)

Name:

_____

Address:

_____

_____

_____

Telephone:

_____

Email:

_____

NOTE: You can also sow your special seed SAFELY & SECURELY online via www.bishopclimate.org

Bishop Climate Ministries is the Healing & Deliverance Ministry founded by Bishop Climate under the anointing and direction of the Holy Spirit. God has anointed Bishop Climate with incredible power to set the captives free. Many people who were unable to get deliverance anywhere else find their freedom as they attend special deliverance sessions conducted through this ministry. The vision of Bishop Climate Ministries is to reach over 1 billion people with the message of deliverance and prosperity, especially in understanding the things of the spirit. Many people are bound because of lack of knowledge and one of the goals of this ministry is to set people free through education.

Child of God I want you to know how much I appreciate you and how special you are to me. That is why God keeps giving me the wisdom to write these books at such a time as this. He sees your heart and wants you to experience the abundant life that Jesus died for. And so do I. Your support for our ministry is crucial and I hope that you will always continue to lift us up in prayer to God.

I want to take this opportunity to encourage you to partner with us at Bishop Climate Ministries. Hundreds have testified of the miracles that have taken place in their life just as a result of sowing into this ministry and I want you to be able to experience that 100 fold return Jesus spoke about regarding sowing seed into good ground. The Bible says in Proverbs 11:24 *"One person gives freely, yet gains even more; another withholds unduly, but comes to poverty"*. Your prayers and financial support are crucial to take this message of salvation and deliverance around the world. And as you do that you can be sure that God is going to bless you beyond your wildest imaginations. There is a 4-fold anointing that you step under when you become a partner with Bishop Climate Ministries. It is the anointing that God has put over my life and this ministry according to Isaiah 11:2. That is the anointing of Divine Direction, Divine Connections, Divine Provision and Divine Protection.

Please understand how much I value you. Your support for our ministry is so crucial and your prayers are as a pillar to us. Your partnership with this ministry is so important and that's why we are committed to praying for you daily and lifting your needs up before God. When you send in your donation please send me a prayer request as well so I can intercede on your behalf before God. I look forward to seeing you in person at our Healing and Deliverance Centre in London, England or at one of our Healing and Deliverance Miracle Crusades.

Remember this is the Ministry where the captives are set free and souls are refreshed.

Remain blessed,

Bishop Climate Irungu

Victory Over The Spirit Of Humiliation &
Oppression
Breaking The Curse Of
Good Beginnings & Bad Endings
Victory Over Demonic Assignments
Overcoming Every Generational Hatred
Overcoming Persistent Enemies
Destroying Every Demonic Blockage
Victory Over Every Troubling Spirit
Destroying Every Spirit of Poverty & Lack
Destroying Every Demonic Covenant Over Your
Life
Victory Over Every Appointment With Death
Binding the Strongman
Victory Over Every Evil Wish
Breaking Every Demonic Spell
Overturning Every Demonic Judgement
Breaking Every Frustrating Spirit
Destroying Every Demonic Altar
Uprooting Every Territorial Sorcerers

Victory Over Demonic Storms (Marine Spirit)
Bringing Down Goliath (Spirit of Fear)
Dealing With the Spirit of Disappointment
Victory Over The Lying Spirit
Casting Out The Spirit of Anger
Breaking The Spirit Of Pride
Destroying Every Demonic Contamination
Burning Every Spirit Of Mockery

Order Enquiries: Please call our offices or order online at www.bishopclimate.me

Bishop Climate Ministries
PO Box 67884
London, England SE5 9JJ
www.bishopclimate.org
Email: prayer@bishopclimate.org
Tel: +44 7984 115900 (UK)
Tel: +44 207 738 3668 (UK)
Tel: +732 444 8943 (USA)

Printed in Poland
by Amazon Fulfillment
Poland Sp. z o.o., Wrocław